7-String Guitar Chord Book

by Chad Johnson

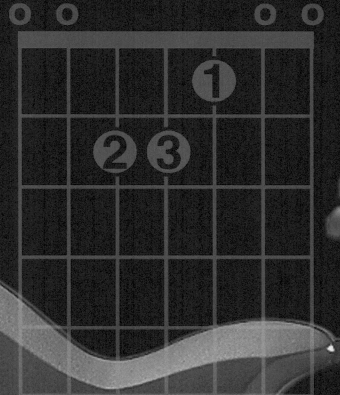

ISBN 978-0-634-03858-7

CORPORATION

7777 W. BLUEMOUND RD. P.O. BOX 13819 MILWAUKEE, WI 53213

Visit Hal Leonard Online at
www.halleonard.com

Table of Contents

Introduction

Although the seven-string guitar may seem like the new kid in the world of the guitar, the instrument has actually been around for centuries—at least two, to be specific. Classical and jazz players have both made use of seven-strings throughout the latter part of the guitar's youthful history. It's certainly arguable, however, that the popularity of the instrument has reached a new height in the past decade. The presence of the seven-string in the world of hard rock has been more than a gimmick; in some instances, it's become an integral and defining element of a band's sound.

One of the first seven-string guitars (of modern design) to appear dates back to the eighteenth century. Andreas O. Sichra (1772–1861) invented the Russian seven-string guitar and composed some seventy-five pieces specifically for the instrument. Several Russian guitarists employed the instrument, creating a healthy repertoire of seven-string Russian classical pieces. Arguably the most influential seven-string player in history, George Van Eps (1913–1998) has been called the "Father of the Seven-String Guitar." Van Eps commissioned Epiphone to build him a seven-string prototype in 1938, and with it he began to redefine the boundaries of solo jazz guitar. Dubbing the instrument his "lap piano," Van Eps made the seven-string his mainstay of musical expression, and he used it extensively during his jazz orchestra gigs (including the Paul Weston Orchestra) and recording sessions. The expanded range of the seven-string granted Van Eps the freedom to develop the beautiful and intricate pianistic voicings for which he would become well known.

The seven-string began to seriously catch on once again during the early nineties. This was in large part due to the virtuoso rock guitarist Steve Vai. Ibanez released a Steve Vai seven-string model (which he used on his 1990 platinum-selling instrumental album *Passion and Warfare*), and the guitar slowly began popping up in the hands of both aspiring young guitarists and seasoned pros alike. Three of those then-aspiring young guitarists, Munky, Head, and Mike Einziger, have gone on to fuel the rhythm section of their multiplatinum bands, Korn and Incubus, respectively, with the seven-string. All three players have cited Steve Vai as a large influence. Other players of note that have made use of the instrument include John Petrucci (Dream Theater) and Wes Borland (Limp Bizkit). This list hardly scratches the surface of the players (now famous and famous-to-be) that have caught the seven-string bug.

The appeal of the seven-string in hard rock and metal stems mainly from the low B string. Years before the seven-string caught on, some bands had already begun the now-common technique of detuning (or tuning down) their instruments in favor of the "heavier" sound it afforded them. With the seven-string, new levels of ultra-low "heaviness" have been achieved, and, believe it or not, some bands have already started *detuning* the seven-string. A jazz guitar virtuoso named Charlie Hunter actually plays an *eight-string* guitar featuring five guitar strings and three bass strings! If you ever feel the need to have your jaw hit the floor, listen to one of his recordings.

The possibilities with the seven-string reach far beyond the extra low B string. Although the instrument has been primarily employed in the riffing styles of rock and metal, the instrument particularly shines in the solo guitar genre. Beyond the possibility of an extra 4th bass range, it's important to note the expanded *relative* range that exists as well. The bass range is made more effective and apparent when contrasted with the treble range. In other words, playing low riffs on the seven– string has the tendency to sound simply like a detuned six-string, whereas exploiting the greater range afforded with the extra string draws attention away from the bass and places it more on the music as a whole. The important thing to remember is that the low B string doesn't *have* to be used in every riff. The effect of the added range can be greatly enhanced if the extra string is put to use only occasionally when needed, rather than during every single phrase.

With that said, it's time to learn how to include the seventh string in the chords you know and love. Again, these are at your disposal; don't feel the need to make every chord in your songs or arrangements a seven-string one. Pick and choose the ones you like, and use the ones you feel the song really needs. Have fun!

How to Use This Book

A fingerboard chart of the seven-string neck is provided below for reference. To expedite the learning of the note names on the seventh string, it's important to remember that you already know (or hopefully know!) the note names on the B string—just two octaves higher. So, if you ever used the technique of learning the two E strings (sixth and first) together, the same can be done for the low B string.

The Seven-String Fingerboard

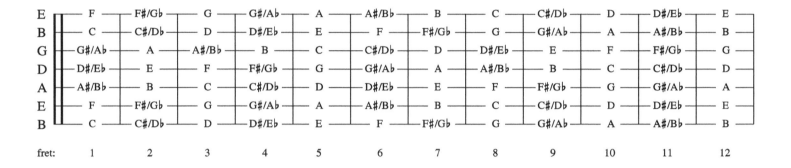

The chords throughout this book are presented in chord grid fashion. In case you're not familiar with this type of notation, below is a detailed explanation of how they're read.

The seven vertical lines represent the strings on the guitar. The lowest string (B) is on the left, moving through to the highest string (E) on the right.

An "o" indicates that the string is played open

The black dots indicate which notes to play, and the numbers indicate the finger to fret with.

The "x" indicates that the string is to be muted or not played at all.

This thick line represents the nut.

The horizontal lines represent frets.

The numbers along the bottom indicate the degree of the chord.

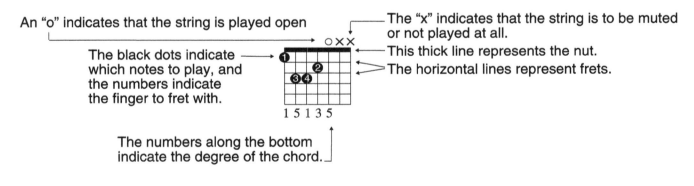

This curved line represents a barre, indicating you should lay the finger flat across the strings.

For chords that are not played in open position, a fret indicator will let you know which position to move to.

Chord Construction

This section is intended to provide a basic knowledge of chords, how to build them, and how to use them. Some of you may already know this; if so, skip ahead. If not, read on and learn how to impress your friends who don't know!

Triads

A chord is simply a collection of notes deliberately arranged in a harmonious (or sometimes nonharmonious) fashion. The most common type of chord is called a *triad*. The name tells the number of notes in the chord—three. Triads can be one of four different *qualities:* major, minor, augmented, or diminished. Below, we find what's known as a C Major triad:

The words *root*, *3rd*, and *5th* below the notes on the staff indicate how each note is functioning within the chord. A root note is the foundation of the chord and the note after which the chord will be named.

Intervals

The other two notes in our C triad (the 3rd and the 5th) are responsible for the quality of the chord. The notes C and E are an *interval* (or distance) of a major 3rd apart. Intervals are comprised of two components: a number and a quality.

We can determine that C to E is a 3rd by simply counting through the musical alphabet. Starting from C: C is one, D is two, and E is three. (The word *root* is many times used interchangeably with the number 1. For all practical purposes, they mean the same thing.) From C to G is a 5th, and we can confirm this by again counting up from C: C(1)–D(2)–E(3)–F(4)–G(5).

Determining the quality of an interval is not quite as easy as the number, but it's not too difficult. It will require a bit of memorization, but it's very logical. Below we'll find all twelve of the notes in the chromatic scale and their intervals measured from a C root note:

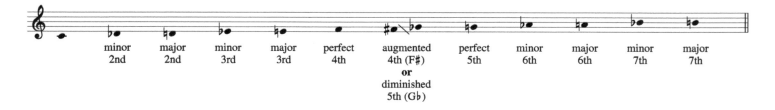

This example tells us a great deal about intervals. We can see a few formulas here at work. The first thing we should notice is that a *minor* interval is always one half step *smaller* than a *major* interval. C to E is a major 3rd, whereas C to E♭ is a minor 3rd. C to A is a major 6th, whereas C to A♭ is a minor 6th, etc. The next thing we should notice is how 4ths and 5ths work. We can see that an *augmented* interval is always one half step *greater* than a *perfect* one, and a *diminished* interval is always one half step *smaller*.

Any triad of one of the four above-mentioned qualities will contain a root, 3rd, and 5th. Other types of triads you may encounter include 6 chords, sus4 chords, and sus2 chords. These chords are the product of (in the case of sus4 and sus2 chords) replacing the 3rd with another note or (in the case of 6 chords) replacing the 5th (or sometimes adding to it) with another note.

Below are several different qualities of triads that will allow us to examine these intervals at work and note how they affect the names of these chords:

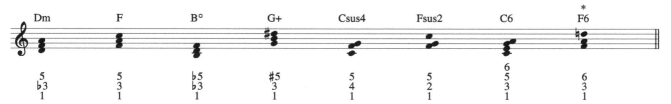

The symbol ° stands for diminished, while the symbol + stands for augmented.
* Note that the 5th tone may or may not be present in a 6 chord.

7th Chords

Beyond the triad, we'll encounter many more chords, most commonly 7th chords. These chords will not only contain the root, 3rd, and 5th, but also the 7th. Below are a few common 7th chords. (Note that the 7th interval can be major or minor independently of the 3rd, thus affecting the name of the chord.)

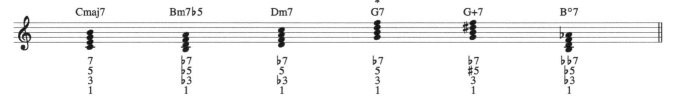

* Note that the G7 chord contains a major 3rd and a minor 7th. This type of chord is referred to as a *dominant 7th*.

Extensions

Finally, beyond 7th chords, we have extensions. The concept of extensions is a bit complicated and will only be touched upon here, as it requires more extensive study than is possible within the scope of this book. Basically, extended chords continue the process of stacking notes onto a triad that we began with the 7th chord. Instead of only adding the 7th to the chord, however, in a 9th chord we'll add the 7th and the 9th. In an 11th chord, we'll add the 7th, 9th, and 11th to our triad, etc. Now, here's the catch: not all of these notes need to be present in order for a chord to be an extension. The general rule is, if the 7th is present, then notes other than the root, 3rd, and 5th are extensions and therefore numbered an octave higher (9, 11, 13). The C13 chord below demonstrates this concept:

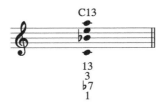

Note that there is no 5th (G) present in this chord, but the presence of the 7th (B♭) tells us that this chord is called C13, rather than some kind of C6 chord.

Again, this section is intended to be a basic tutorial on the concept of chord construction and chord theory. If you're interested in furthering your knowledge on this subject (and I recommend it), I suggest you take a look at some of the many books dedicated to this subject. So, without further ado, let's learn how to play these things!

C

1 5 1 3 5 1 3   1 1 3 5   1 3 5 1

Cm

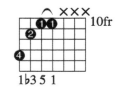

1 5 1♭3   1 1 5 ♭3   1♭3 5 1

C+

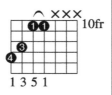
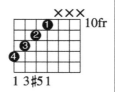

1♯5 1 3♯5 1   1♯5 1 3   1 3♯5 1

C°

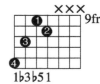

1♭5 1♭3   1 1♭5 ♭3   1♭3♭5 1

C5

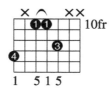

1 5 1   1 5 1 5   1 5 1 5

Cadd9

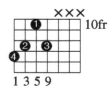

1 1 3 5 9   1 1 9 5 1 3   1 3 5 9

Cm(add9)

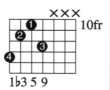

1 1♭3 5 9   1 1 9 5♭3   1♭3 5 9

Csus4

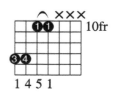

1 1 4 5 1   1 4 1 5 1   1 4 5 1

Csus2

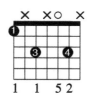
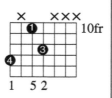

1 5 1 2   1 1 5 2   1 5 2

C6

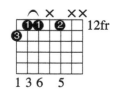

1 5 6 3   1 6 3 5   1 3 6 5

Cm6

  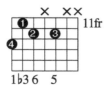

1　6b35 1　　　1 5　b36　　　1b36　5

Cmaj7

  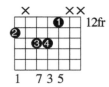

1 51 3 5 7 3　　1 5　3 7　　1　7 3 5

Cmaj7#5

  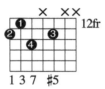

1　1 3#57 3　　1#5　3 7　　1 3 7　#5

Cmaj7b5

  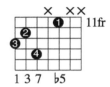

1　3　7b5　　1b5　3　7 3　　1 3 7　b5

Cmaj9

  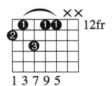

1 5　9 5 7 3　　1　7 3 5 9　　1 3 7 9 5

Cm7

  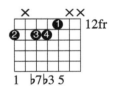

1 5 1b3b7　　1 5　b7 b3　　1　b7b3 5

Cm(maj7)

  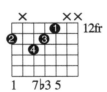

1 5 1b3 7　　1 5　　7b3　　1　7b3 5

Cm7b5

  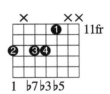

1b5 1b3 b7　　1b5　b7 b3　　1　b7b3b5

Cm9

  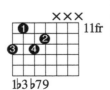

1 5　b3 b79　　1 5 9b3b7　　1b3 b79

Cm11

  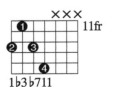

1 5b711　b3　　1 11b7b3 b79　　1b3 b711

9

C7

  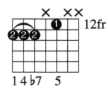

1 5   3 ♭7   1   3 ♭7   5   1 3 ♭7   5

C7sus4

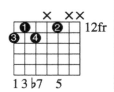

1 5   4 ♭7   1   4 ♭7   5   1 4 ♭7   5

C+7

  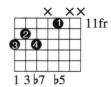

1#5   3 ♭7   1   3 ♭7   #5   1 3 ♭7   #5

C7♭5

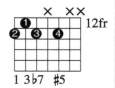

1 ♭5   3 ♭7   1   3 ♭7   ♭5   1 3 ♭7   ♭5

C9

  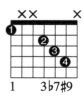

1 5   ♭7 9 3   1   3 ♭7 9 5   1 3 ♭7 9 5

C7♯9

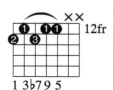 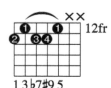

1   3 ♭7#9   1   ♭7 3   #9   1 3 ♭7#9 5

C7♭9

 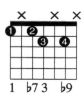 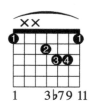

1   3 ♭7♭9   1   ♭7 3   ♭9   1 3 ♭7♭9

C11

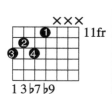 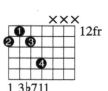

1   3 ♭7 9 11   1 11 ♭7 3 ♭7 9   1 3 ♭7 11

C13

 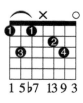

1   ♭7 3 13   1 5 ♭7   13 9   3   1 3 ♭7 9 13

C°7

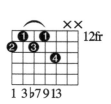 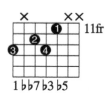

1♭5♭♭7♭3   1♭5   ♭3♭♭7   1♭♭7♭3 ♭5

D♭

D♭

1 5 1 3   1   1   1 3 5   1 3 5 1

D♭m
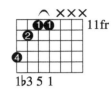

1 5 1♭3   1   ♭3 5 1♭3   1♭3 5 1

D♭+
 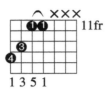 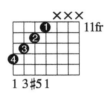

1♯5 1 3♯5 1   1♯5 1 3   1 3♯5 1

D♭°
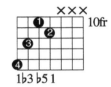 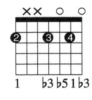

1   ♭3♭5 1♭3   1   1♭5   ♭3   1♭3♭5 1

D♭5
 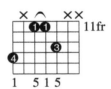

1 5 1   1 5 1   5   1   5 1 5

D♭add9
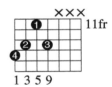

1 5   3   9   1   9 5 1 3   1 3 5 9

D♭m(add9)
 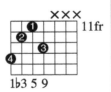

1 5   ♭3   9   1♭3   9 5   1♭3 5 9

D♭sus4
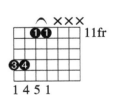 

1 5   4   1 4   1 4 1   5   1 4 5 1

D♭sus2
 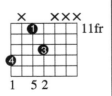 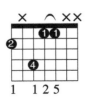

1 5 1 2   1   1 2 5   1   5 2

D♭6
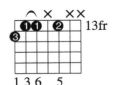

1 5 6 3   1   6 3 5   1 3 6   5

D♭m6

1 6 5 1 b3   1 5 b3 6   1b36   5

D♭maj7

  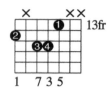

1 1 3 5 7 3   1 5   3 7   1   7 3 5

D♭maj7♯5

  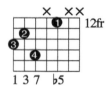

1 1 3#5 7 3   1#5   3 7   1 3 7   #5

D♭maj7♭5

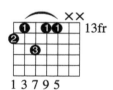 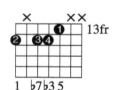

1 1 3b5 7 3   1   3 7 b5   1 3 7   b5

D♭maj9

 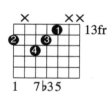

1 5 9 5 7 3   1   7 3 9   1 3 7 9 5

D♭m7

  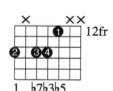

1 1b3b7b7b3   1 5   b7b3   1 b7b3 5

D♭m(maj7)

 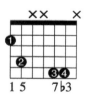

1 5 1b3 7   1 5   7b3   1   7b3 5

D♭m7♭5

  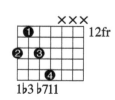

1 1b3b5b7b3   1b5   b7b3   1 b7b3b5

D♭m9

  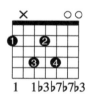

1 5 b3b7 9   1b3   9 5b7b3   1b3b7 9

D♭m11

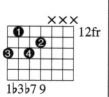 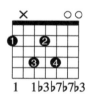

1 5b711   b3   1 11b7b3b79   1b3 b711

D♭7

  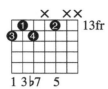

1 5 3 ♭7   1   3 ♭7 5   1 3 ♭7 5

D♭7sus4

  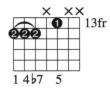

1 5 4 ♭7   1   4 ♭7 5   1 4 ♭7 5

D♭+7

  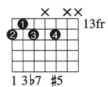

1 #5 3 ♭7   1   3 ♭7 #5   1 3 ♭7 #5

D♭7♭5

 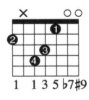 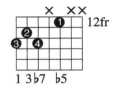

1   3 ♭5 ♭7   1   3 ♭7 ♭5   1 3 ♭7 ♭5

D♭9

1 5 ♭7 3 9   1   3 ♭7 9 5   1 3 ♭7 9 5

D♭7#9

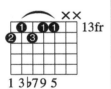 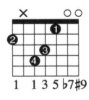 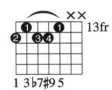

1 1 3 5 ♭7 #9   1 ♭7 3   #9   1 3 ♭7 #9 5

D♭7♭9

 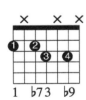

1   3 ♭7 ♭9   1 ♭7 3   ♭9   1 3 ♭7 ♭9

D♭11

 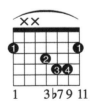 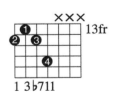

1   3 ♭7 9 11   1 11 ♭7 3 ♭7 9   1 3 ♭7 11

D♭13

  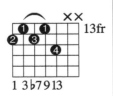

1   ♭7 3 13   1 5 ♭7 3 13 9   1 3 ♭7 9 13

D♭°7

  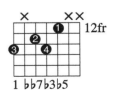

1   ♭♭7 ♭5 1 ♭3 1 ♭5 ♭3 ♭♭7   1 ♭♭7 ♭3 ♭5

D

D

1 5 1 5 1 3

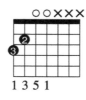
1 1 3 5

1 3 5 1

Dm

1 5 1 5 1 b3

1 5 b3 5 1

1 b3 5 1

D+

1 #5 3 1

1 1 3 #5

1 3 #5 1

D°

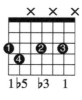
1 b5 b3 1

1 1 b5 1 b3

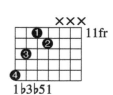
11fr
1 b3 b5 1

D5

1 5 1 5 1

1 5 1

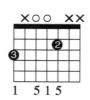
1 5 1 5

Dadd9

1 5 3 5 1 9

1 1 3 5 1 9

1 3 5 9

Dm(add9)

1 5 b3 5 1 9

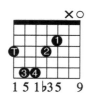
1 5 1 b3 5 9

1 b3 5 9

Dsus4

1 5 1 5 1 4

1 1 1 4 1 5

1 4 5 1

Dsus2

1 5 1 5 1 2

1 5 2 5 1

1 5 2

D6

1 5 1 6 1 3

1 3 6 1

1 3 6 5

Dm6

1 5 1 5 6b3   1   b3 6 1   1b3 6   5

Dmaj7

1 5 1 5 7 3   1 5 3 5 7   1 7 3 5

Dmaj7#5

1   1#5 7 3   1 7 3#5   1 3 7 #5

Dmaj7b5

1   1b5 7 3   1 7 3 b5   1 3 7 b5

Dmaj9

1 5 3 5 7 9   1 5 9 5 7 3   1 3 7 9 5

Dm7

1 5 1 5b7b3   1 5 1 b3b7 1   1 b7b3 5

Dm(maj7)

 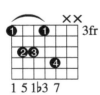

1 5 1 5 7b3   1 5 1b3 7   1 7b3 5

Dm7b5

1   1b5b7b3   1b5 1 b3b7   1 b7b3b5

Dm9

 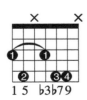

1 5b3 5b7 9   1 5 b3b7 9   1b3b7 9

Dm11

 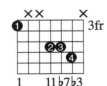

1 5b3 11b7 9   1 11b7b3   1b3b7 11

D7

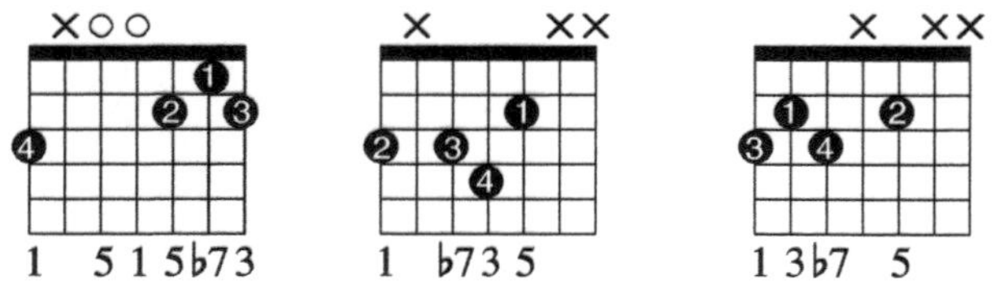
1 5 1 5 ♭7 3
1 ♭7 3 5
1 3 ♭7 5

D7sus4

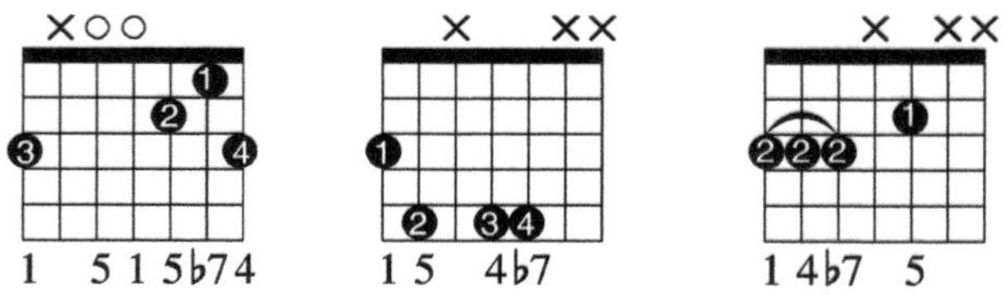
1 5 1 5 ♭7 4
1 5 4 ♭7
1 4 ♭7 5

D+7

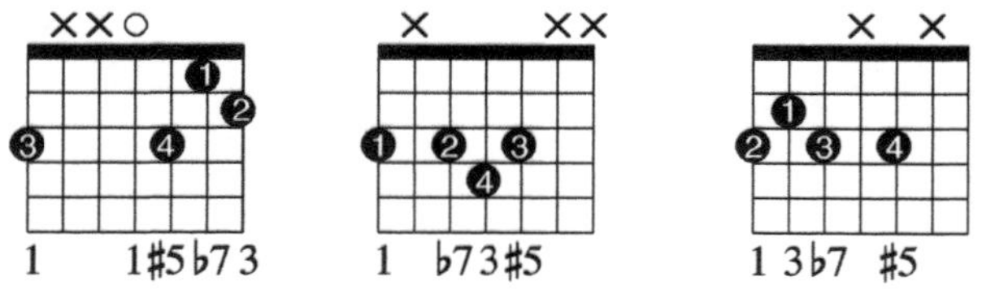
1 1 ♯5 ♭7 3
1 ♭7 3 ♯5
1 3 ♭7 ♯5

D7♭5

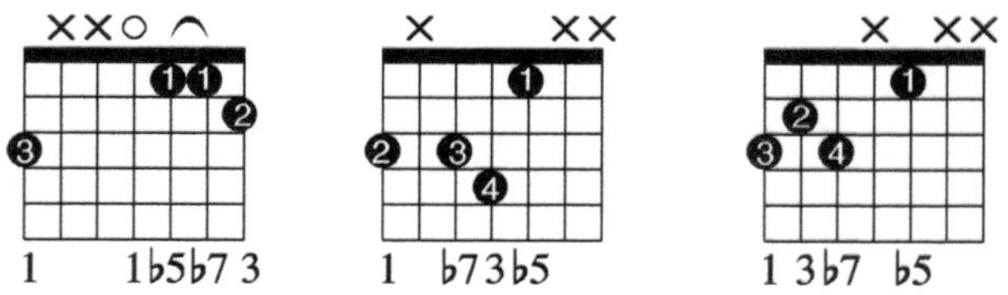
1 1 ♭5 ♭7 3
1 ♭7 3 ♭5
1 3 ♭7 ♭5

D9

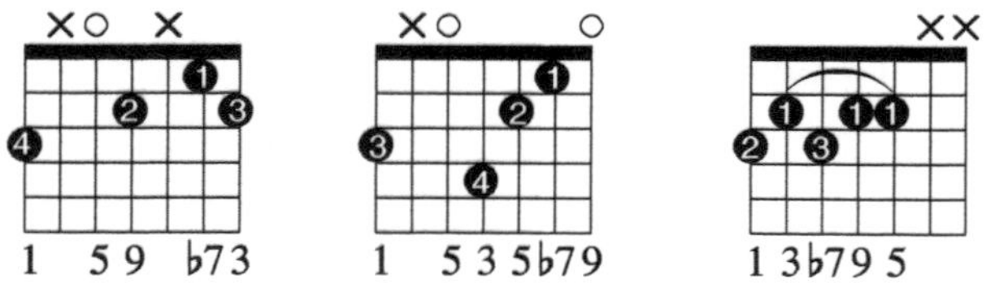
1 5 9 ♭7 3
1 5 3 5 ♭7 9
1 3 ♭7 9 5

D7♯9

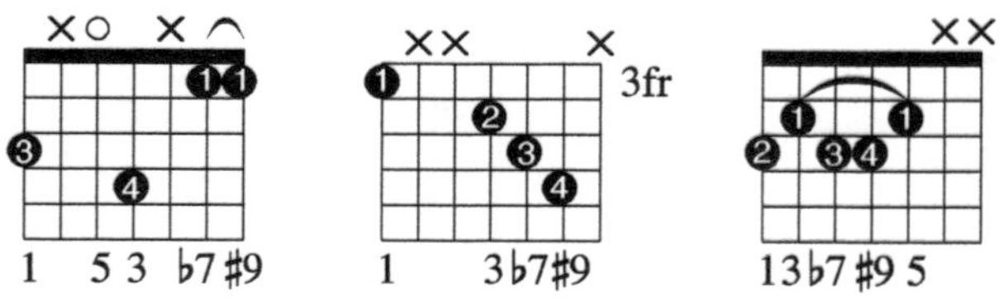
1 5 3 ♭7 ♯9
3fr
1 3 ♭7 ♯9
1 3 ♭7 ♯9 5

D7♭9

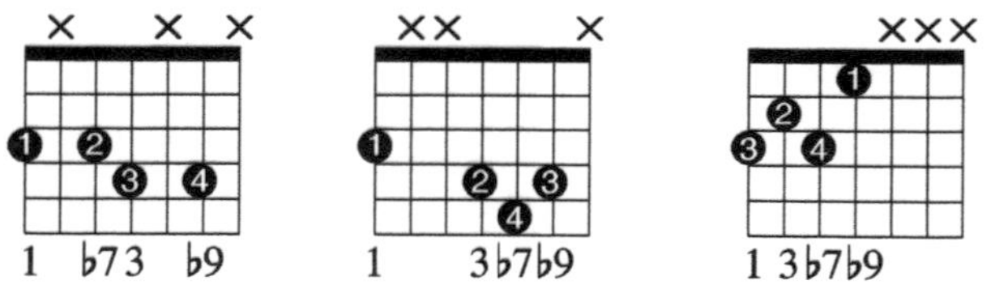
1 ♭7 3 ♭9
1 3 ♭7 ♭9
1 3 ♭7 ♭9

D11

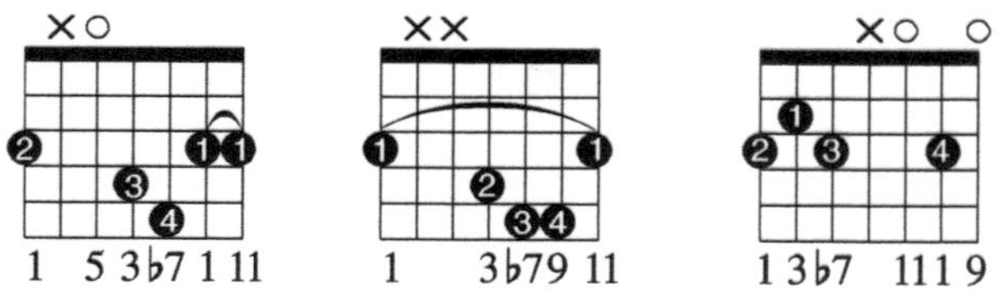
1 5 3 ♭7 1 11
1 3 ♭7 9 11
1 3 ♭7 11 1 9

D13

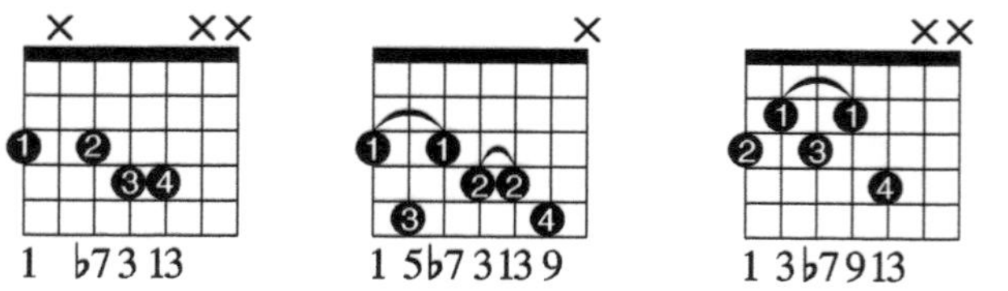
1 ♭7 3 13
1 5 ♭7 3 13 9
1 3 ♭7 9 13

D°7

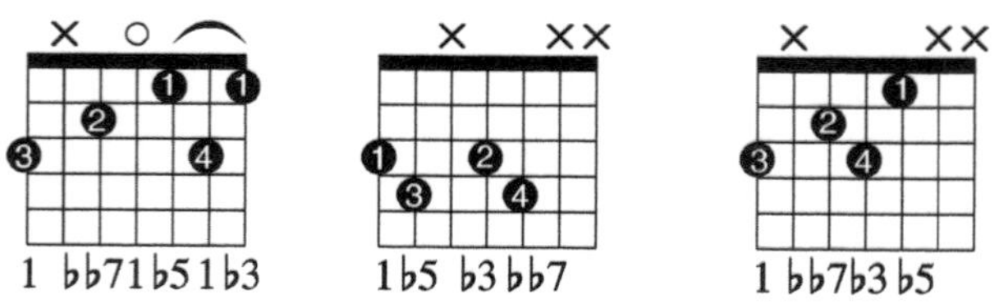
1 ♭♭7 1 ♭5 1 ♭3
1 ♭5 ♭3 ♭♭7
1 ♭♭7 ♭3 ♭5

E♭

E♭
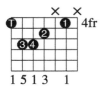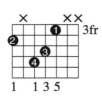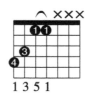

1 5 1 3 1   1 1 3 5   1 3 5 1

E♭m
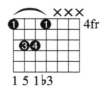

1 5 1♭3   1 1 5 ♭3   1♭3 5 1

E♭+

1 #5 1 3 #5 1   1 #5 1 3   1 3 #5 1

E♭°

1♭5 1♭3   1 1♭5 ♭3   1♭3♭5 1

E♭5

1 5 1   1 5 1 5   1 5 1 5

E♭add9
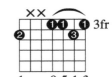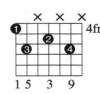

1 5 3 9   1 9 5 1 3   1 3 5 9

E♭m(add9)
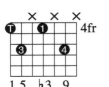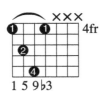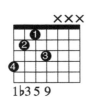

1 5 ♭3 9   1 5 9 ♭3   1♭3 5 9

E♭sus4
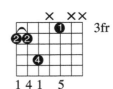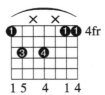

1 5 4 1 4   1 4 1 5   1 4 5 1

E♭sus2
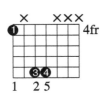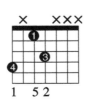

1 5 1 2   1 2 5   1 5 2

E♭6
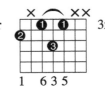

1 5 6 3   1 6 3 5   1 3 6 5

E♭m6

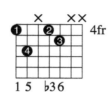 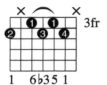

E♭maj7

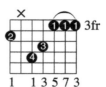

E♭maj7♯5

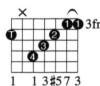 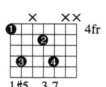

E♭maj7♭5

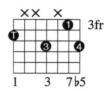 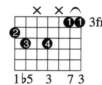

E♭maj9

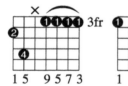 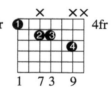

E♭m7

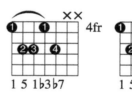 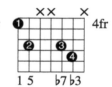

E♭m(maj7)

 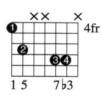

E♭m(7♭5)

 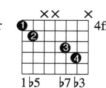

E♭m9

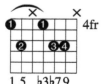 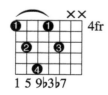

E♭m11

 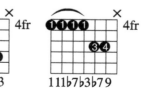 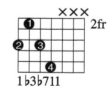

E♭7

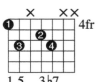 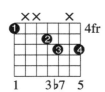

1 5 3 ♭7   1 3 ♭7 5   1 3 ♭7 5

E♭7sus4

 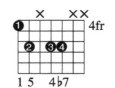 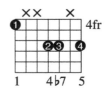

1 5 4 ♭7   1 4 ♭7 5   1 4 ♭7 5

E♭+7

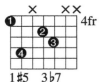 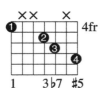

1 #5 3 ♭7   1 3 ♭7 #5   1 3 ♭7 #5

E♭7♭5

 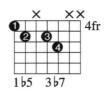 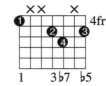

1 ♭5 3 ♭7   1 3 ♭7 ♭5   1 3 ♭7 ♭5

E♭9

1 5 ♭7 3   9   1 3 ♭7 9 5   1 3 ♭7 9 5

E♭7#9

 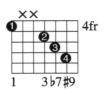 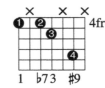

1 3 ♭7 #9   1 ♭7 3 #9   1 3 ♭7 #9 5

E♭7♭9

 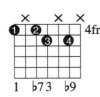 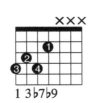

1 3 ♭7 ♭9   1 ♭7 3 ♭9   1 3 ♭7 ♭9

E♭11

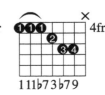 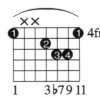 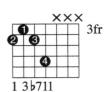

1 3 ♭7 9 11   1 11 ♭7 3 ♭7 9   1 3 ♭7 11

E♭13

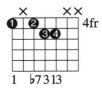 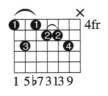

1 ♭7 3 13   1 5 ♭7 3 13 9   1 3 ♭7 9 13

E♭°7

 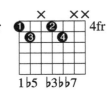

1 ♭5 ♭♭7 ♭3   1 ♭5 ♭3 ♭♭7   1 ♭♭7 ♭3 ♭5

E

E

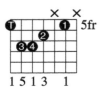 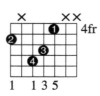

1 5 1 3　1　　1　　1 3 5　　　5 1 5 1 3 5 1

Em

 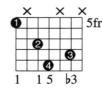

1 5 1♭3　　1　　1 5　♭3　　　5 1 5 1♭35 1

E+

 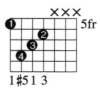 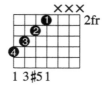

1♯5 1 3♯5 1　　1♯5 1 3　　　1 3♯5 1

E°

 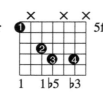

1♭5 1♭3　　1　1♭5　♭3　　　1♭3♭5 1

E5

1 5 1　　1 5 1 5　　　1　5 1 5

Eadd9

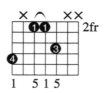 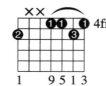 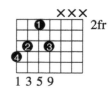

1 5　3　9　　1　9 5 1 3　　　1 3 5 9

Em(add9)

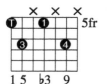 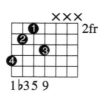 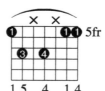

1 5　♭3　9　　1 5 9♭3　　　1♭3 5 9

Esus4

  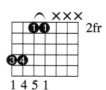

1 5　4　1 4　　1 4 1　5　　　1 4 5 1

Esus2

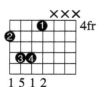 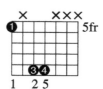 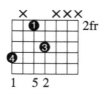

1 5 1 2　　1　2 5　　　1　5 2

E6

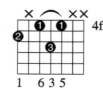 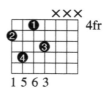 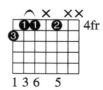

1 5 6 3　　1　6 3 5　　　1 3 6　5

Em6

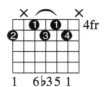 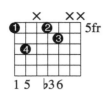 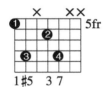

1   6 b3 5 1   1 5 b3 6   1 b3 6   5

Emaj7

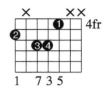 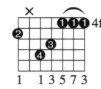 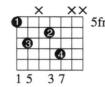

1 1 3 5 7 3   1 5 3 7   1 7 3 5

Emaj7#5

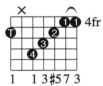 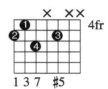 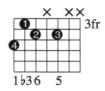

1 1 3 #5 7 3   1 #5 3 7   1 3 7   #5

Emaj7b5

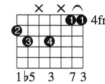 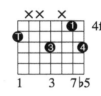 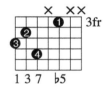

1   3 7 b5   1 b5 3 7 3   1 3 7   b5

Emaj9

  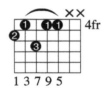

1 5 9 5 7 3   1 7 3 9   1 3 7 9 5

Em7

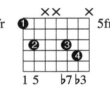 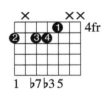

1 5 1 b3 b7   1 5   b7 b3   1 b7 b3 5

Em(maj7)

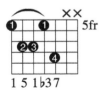 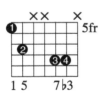 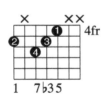

1 5 1 b3 7   1 5   7 b3   1 7 b3 5

Em7b5

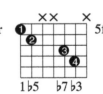 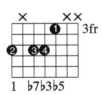

1 b5 1 b3 b7   1 b5 b7 b3   1 b7 b3 b5

Em9

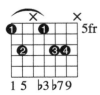 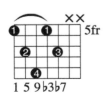 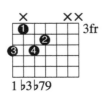

1 5 b3 b7 9   1 5 9 b3 b7   1 b3 b7 9

Em11

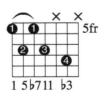 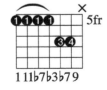 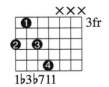

1 5 b7 11 b3   1 11 b7 b3 b7 9   1 b3 b7 11

E7

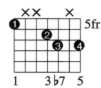

1 5   3 b7   1   3 b7 5   1 3 b7   5

E7sus4

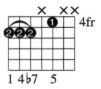

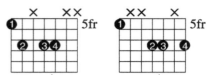

1 5   4 b7   1   4 b7 5   1 4 b7   5

E+7

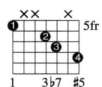
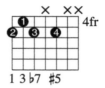

1 #5   3 b7   1   3 b7 #5   1 3 b7 #5

E7b5

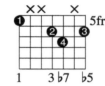
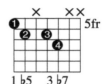
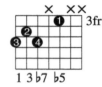

1 b5   3 b7   1   3 b7 b5   1 3 b7 b5

E9

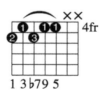

1 5 b7 3 9   1   3 b7 9 5   1 3 b7 9 5

E7#9

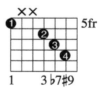
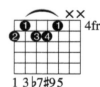

1   3 b7 #9   1 b7 3 #9   1 3 b7 #9 5

E7b9

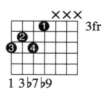
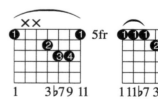

1   3 b7 b9   1 b7 3 b9   1 3 b7 b9

E11

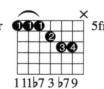

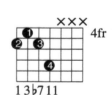

1   3 b7 9 11   1 11 b7 3 b7 9   1 3 b7 11

E13

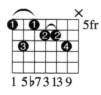
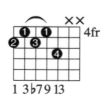

1 b7 3 13   1 5 b7 3 13 9   1 3 b7 9 13

E°7

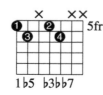
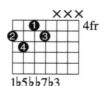
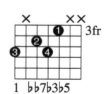

1 b5 bb7 b3   1 b5 b3 bb7   1 bb7 b3 b5

F

F

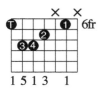
6fr
1 5 1 3　1

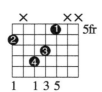
5fr
1　1 3 5

3fr
1 3 5 1

Fm

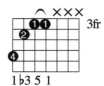
6fr
1 5 1♭3

6fr
1　1 5　♭3

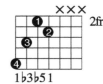
3fr
1♭3 5 1

F+

6fr
1♯5 1 3♯5 1

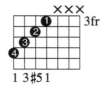
6fr
1♯5 1 3

3fr
1 3♯5 1

F°

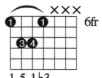
6fr
1♭5 1♭3

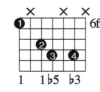
6fr
1　1♭5　♭3

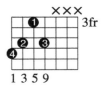
2fr
1♭3♭5 1

F5

6fr
1 5 1

6fr
1 5 1 5

3fr
1　5 1 5

Fadd9

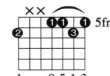
6fr
1 5　3　9

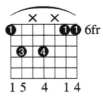
5fr
1　9 5 1 3

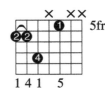
3fr
1 3 5 9

Fm(add9)

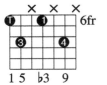
6fr
1 5　♭3　9

6fr
1 5 9♭3

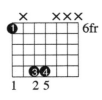
3fr
1♭3 5 9

Fsus4

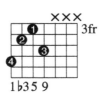
6fr
1 5　4　1 4

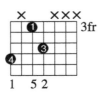
5fr
1 4 1　5

3fr
1 4 5 1

Fsus2

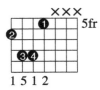
5fr
1 5 1 2

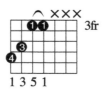
6fr
1　2 5

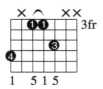
3fr
1　5 2

F6

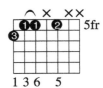
5fr
1 5 6 3

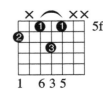
5fr
1　6 3 5

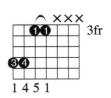
5fr
1 3 6　5

23

Fm6

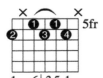 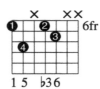 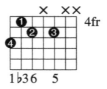

1 6 b3 5 1   1 5 b3 6   1 b3 6 5

Fmaj7

 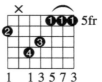 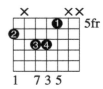

1 1 3 5 7 3   1 5 3 7   1 7 3 5

Fmaj7#5

 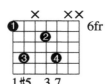 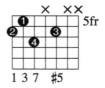

1 1 3 #5 7 3   1 #5 3 7   1 3 7 #5

Fmaj7b5

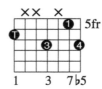 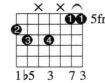 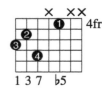

1 3 7 b5   1 b5 3 7 3   1 3 7 b5

Fmaj9

 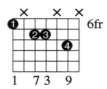 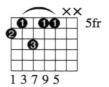

1 5 9 5 7 3   1 7 3 9   1 3 7 9 5

Fm7

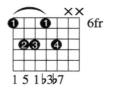 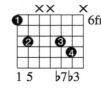 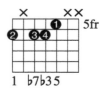

1 5 1 b3 b7   1 5 b7 b3   1 b7 b3 5

Fm(maj7)

  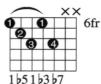

1 5 1 b3 7   1 5 7 b3   1 7 b3 5

Fm7b5

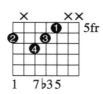 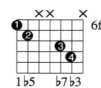 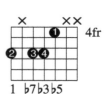

1 b5 1 b3 b7   1 b5 b7 b3   1 b7 b3 b5

Fm9

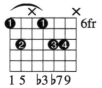 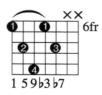 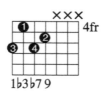

1 5 b3 b7 9   1 5 9 b3 b7   1 b3 b7 9

Fm11

 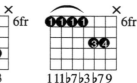 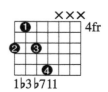

1 5 b7 11 b3   1 11 b7 b3 b7 9   1 b3 b7 11

F7

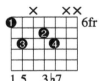 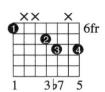 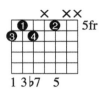

F7sus4

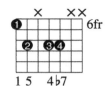 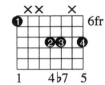 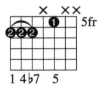

F+7

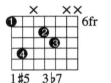 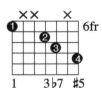 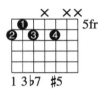

F7♭5

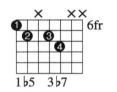 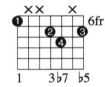 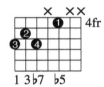

F9

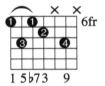 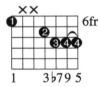 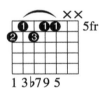

F7♯9

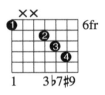 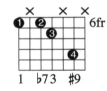 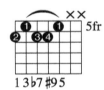

F7♭9

 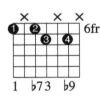 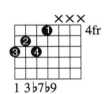

F11

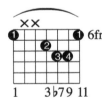 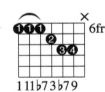 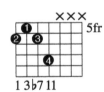

F13

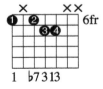 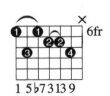 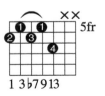

F°7

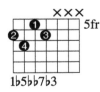 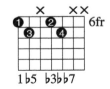 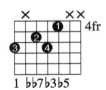

F#

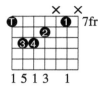 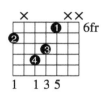

1 5 1 3   1   1   1 3 5   1 3 5 1

F#m

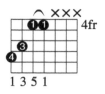 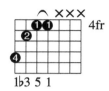

1 5 1b3   1   1 5   b3   1b3 5 1

F#+

 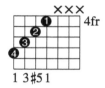 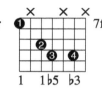

1#5 1 3#5 1   1#5 1 3   1 3#5 1

F#°

 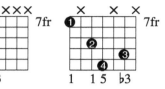 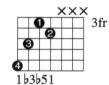

1b5 1b3   1   1b5   b3   1b3b5 1

F#5

  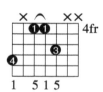

1 5 1   1 5 1 5   1   5 1 5

F#add9

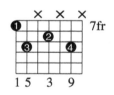 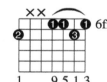 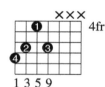

1 5   3   9   1   9 5 1 3   1 3 5 9

F#m(add9)

  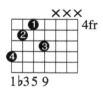

1 5   b3   9   1 5 9b3   1b3 5 9

F#sus4

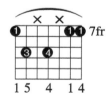 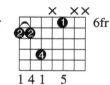 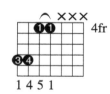

1 5   4   1 4   1 4 1   5   1 4 5 1

F#sus2

 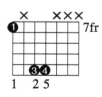 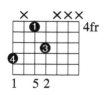

1 5 1 2   1   2 5   1   5 2

F#6

 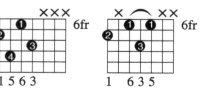 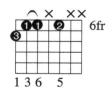

1 5 6 3   1   6 3 5   1 3 6   5

F#m6

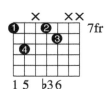

1 6 b3 5 1   1 5   b3 6   1 b3 6   5

F#maj7

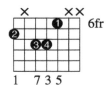

1 1 3 5 7 3   1 5   3 7   1   7 3 5

F#maj7#5

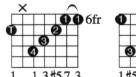

1 1 3 #5 7 3   1 #5   3 7   1 3 7   #5

F#maj7♭5

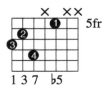

1   3   7 b5   1 b5   3 7 3   1 3 7   b5

F#maj9

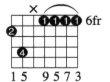

1 5   9 5 7 3   1   7 3   9   1 3 7 9 5

F#m7

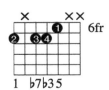

1 5 1 b3 b7   1 5   b7 b3   1   b7 b3 5

F#m(maj7)

1 5 1 b3 7   1 5   7 b3   1   7 b3 5

F#m7♭5

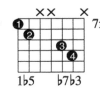

1 b5 1 b3 b7   1 b5   b7 b3   1   b7 b3 b5

F#m9

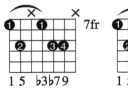

1 5   b3 b7 9   1 5 9 b3 b7   1 b3 b7 9

F#m11

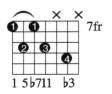

1 5 b7 11   b3   1 11 b7 b3 b7 9   1 b3 b7 11

F#7

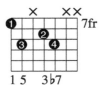 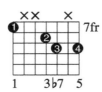 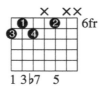

1 5 3b7   1 3b7 5   1 3b7 5

F#7sus4

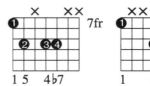 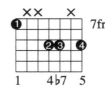 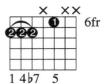

1 5 4b7   1 4b7 5   1 4b7 5

F#+7

 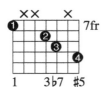 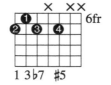

1#5 3b7   1 3b7 #5   1 3b7 #5

F#7b5

 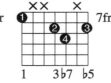 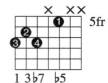

1b5 3b7   1 3b7 b5   1 3b7 b5

F#9

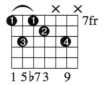 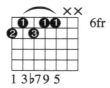

1 5b73 9   1 3b79 5   1 3b79 5

F#7#9

 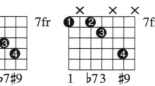 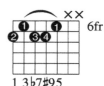

1 3b7#9   1 b73 #9   1 3b7#95

F#7b9

  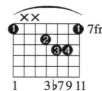

1 3b7b9   1 b73 b9   1 3b7b9

F#11

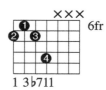 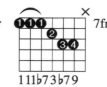 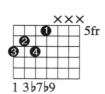

1 3b79 11   111b73b79   1 3b711

F#13

 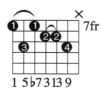 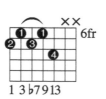

1 b7313   1 5b73139   1 3b7913

F#°7

 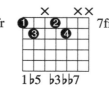 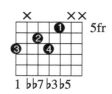

1b5bb7b3   1b5 b3bb7   1 bb7b3b5

G

G

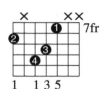

1 5 1 3   1   1   1 3 5   5 1 3 5 1 3 1

Gm

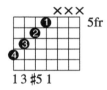

1 5 1b3   1   1 5 b3   1b3 5 1

G+
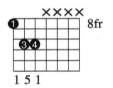
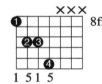

1#5 1 3#5 1   1#5 1 3   1 3 #5 1

G°
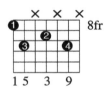
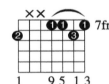
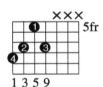

1b5 1b3   1 1b5 b3   1b3b51

G5

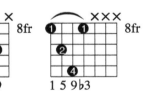
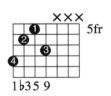

1 5 1   1 5 1 5   5 1 5 1 5 1

Gadd9
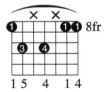

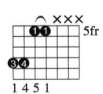

1 5 3 9   1 9 5 1 3   1 3 5 9

Gm(add9)

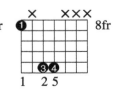
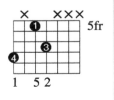

1 5 b3 9   1 5 9b3   1b3 5 9

Gsus4

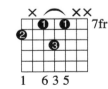
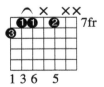

1 5 4 1 4   1 4 1 5   1 4 5 1

Gsus2
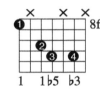

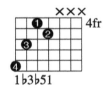

1 5 1 2   1 2 5   1 5 2

G6
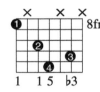
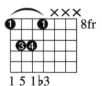
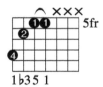

1 5 6 3   1 6 3 5   1 3 6 5

Gm6

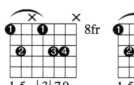 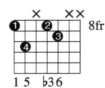 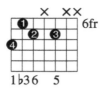

1　6♭3 5 1　　　1 5　♭3 6　　　1♭3 6　　5

Gmaj7

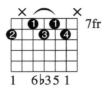 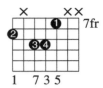

1　1 3 5 7 3　　1 5　　3 7　　　1　7 3 5

Gmaj7♯5

 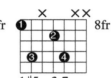 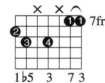

1　1 3♯5 7 3　　1♯5　　3 7　　1 3 7　♯5

Gmaj7♭5

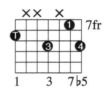 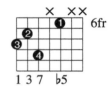 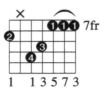

1　　3　7♭5　　1♭5　3　7 3　　1 3 7　♭5

Gmaj9

 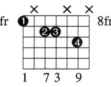 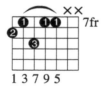

1 5　9 5 7 3　　1　7 3　9　　1 3 7 9 5

Gm7

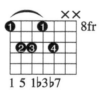 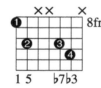 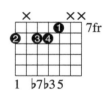

1 5 1♭3♭7　　1 5　♭7♭3　　1　♭7♭3 5

Gm(maj7)

 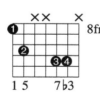

1 5 1♭3 7　　1 5　　7♭3　　1　7♭3 5

Gm7♭5

 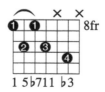 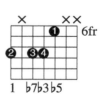

1♭5 1♭3♭7　　1♭5　♭7♭3　　1　♭7♭3♭5

Gm9

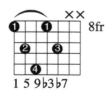 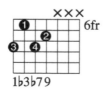 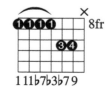

1 5　♭3♭7 9　　1 5　9♭3♭7　　1♭3♭7 9

Gm11

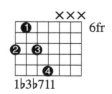

1　5♭7 11　♭3　　1 11♭7♭3♭7 9　　1♭3♭7 11

30

G7

8fr

1 5   3♭7

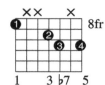
8fr

1   3 ♭7 5

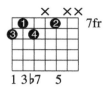
7fr

1 3♭7   5

G7sus4

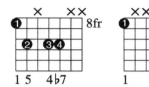
8fr

1 5   4♭7

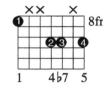
8fr

1   4♭7 5

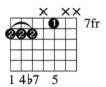
7fr

1 4♭7 5

G+7

8fr

1 #5   3♭7

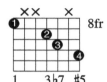
8fr

1   3♭7 #5

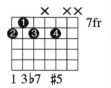
7fr

1 3♭7 #5

G7♭5

8fr

1♭5   3♭7

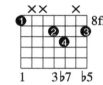
8fr

1   3♭7 ♭5

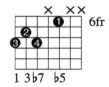
6fr

1 3♭7 ♭5

G9

8fr

1 5♭73   9

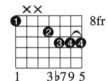
8fr

1   3♭79 5

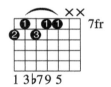
7fr

1 3♭79 5

G7♯9

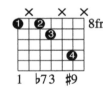
8fr

1   3♭7#9

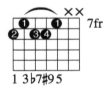
8fr

1   ♭73   #9

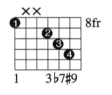
7fr

1 3♭7#9 5

G7♭9

8fr

1   3♭7♭9

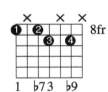
8fr

1   ♭73   ♭9

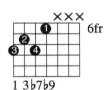
6fr

1 3♭7♭9

G11

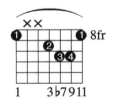
8fr

1   3♭7911

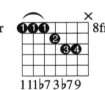
8fr

1 11♭73♭79

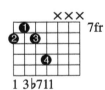
7fr

1 3♭711

G13

8fr

1   ♭7313

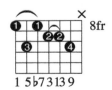
8fr

1 5♭73139

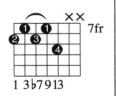
7fr

1 3♭7913

G°7

7fr

1♭5♭♭7♭3

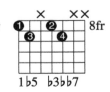
8fr

1♭5   ♭3♭♭7

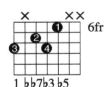
6fr

1 ♭♭7♭3 ♭5

A♭

A♭
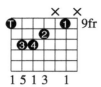 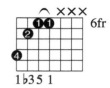

1 5 1 3 1   1 1 3 5   1 3 5 1

A♭m
 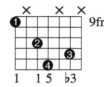 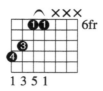

1 5 1♭3   1 1 5 ♭3   1♭3 5 1

A♭+
 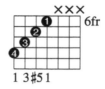

1♯5 1 3♯5 1   1♯5 1 3   1 3♯5 1

A♭°
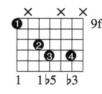 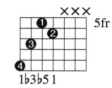 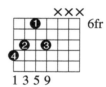

1♭5 1♭3   1 1♭5 ♭3   1♭3♭5 1

A♭5

1 5 1   1 5 1 5   1 5 1 5

A♭add9
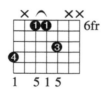 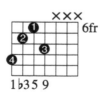 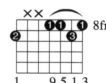

1 5 3 9   1 9 5 1 3   1 3 5 9

A♭m(add9)
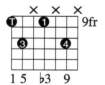 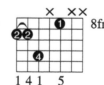

1 5 ♭3 9   1 5 9 ♭3   1♭3 5 9

A♭sus4
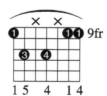 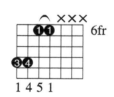 (third)

1 5 4 1 4   1 4 1 5   1 4 5 1

A♭sus2
 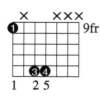 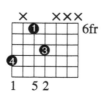

1 5 1 2   1 2 5   1 5 2

A♭6
 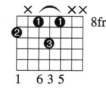 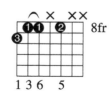

1 5 6 3   1 6 3 5   1 3 6 5

A♭m6

× ⌒ ×
8fr
1　6♭35 1

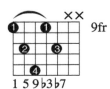
× ××
9fr
1 5　♭36

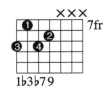
× ××
7fr
1♭36　5

A♭maj7

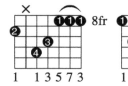
× ⌒
8fr
1　13573

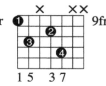
× ××
9fr
1 5　37

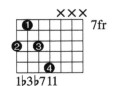
× ××
8fr
1　735

A♭maj7#5

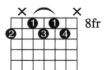
× ⌒
8fr
1　13#573

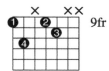
× ××
9fr
1#5　37

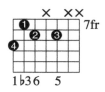
× ××
8fr
137　#5

A♭maj7♭5

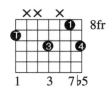
×× ×
8fr
1　3 7♭5

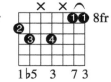
× × ⌒
8fr
1♭5　3 73

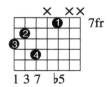
× ××
7fr
137　♭5

A♭maj9

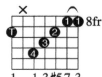
× ⌒
8fr
1 5　95 73

× × ×
9fr
1　73 9

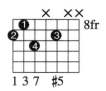
⌒ ××
8fr
1379 5

A♭m7

⌒ ××
9fr
1 5 1♭3♭7

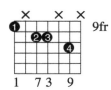
×× ×
9fr
1 5　♭7♭3

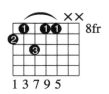
× ××
8fr
1　♭7♭35

A♭m(maj7)

⌒ ××
9fr
1 5 1♭37

×× ×
9fr
1 5　7♭3

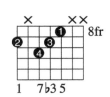
× ××
8fr
1　7♭35

A♭m7♭5

⌒ ××
9fr
1♭51♭3♭7

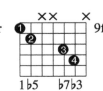
×× ×
9fr
1♭5　♭7♭3

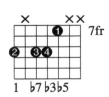
× ××
7fr
1　♭7♭3♭5

A♭m9

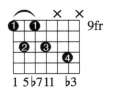
⌒× ×
9fr
1 5　♭3♭79

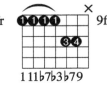
⌒ ××
9fr
1 5 9♭3♭7

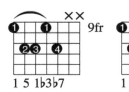
×××
7fr
1♭3♭79

A♭m11

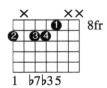
⌒× ×
9fr
1 5♭711　♭3

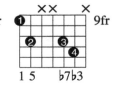
⌒ ×
9fr
1 11♭7♭3♭79

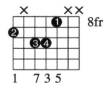
×××
7fr
1♭3♭711

A♭7

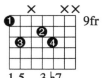
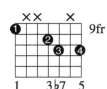

1 5 3 ♭7   1 3♭7 5   1 3♭7 5

A♭7sus4

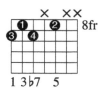
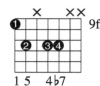
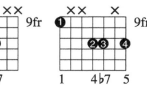

1 5 4♭7   1 4♭7 5   1 4♭7 5

A♭+7

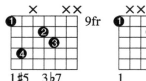
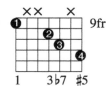

1 ♯5 3♭7   1 3♭7 ♯5   1 3♭7 ♯5

A♭7♭5

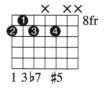
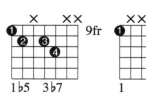
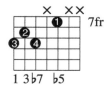

1♭5 3♭7   1 3♭7 ♭5   1 3♭7 ♭5

A♭9

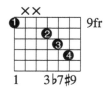

1 5♭73 9   1 3♭79 5   1 3♭79 5

A♭7♯9

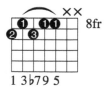
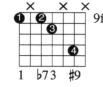
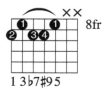

1 3♭7♯9   1 ♭73 ♯9   1 3♭7♯9 5

A♭7♭9

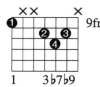
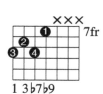
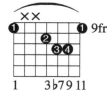

1 3♭7♭9   1 ♭73 ♭9   1 3♭7♭9

A♭11

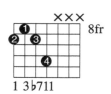

1 3♭79 11   1 11♭73 ♭79   1 3♭711

A♭13

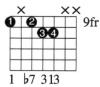
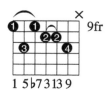
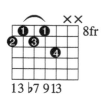

1 ♭7 3 13   1 5♭73 13 9   13 ♭7 9 13

A♭°7

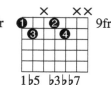
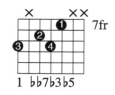

1♭5♭♭7♭3   1♭5 ♭3♭♭7   1 ♭♭7♭3♭5

A

A

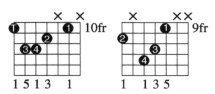

1 5 1 3 1   1 1 3 5   3 5 1 5 1 3 5

Am

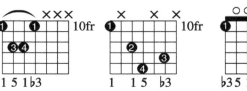

1 5 1 b3   1 1 5 b3   b3 5 1 5 1 b3 5

A+

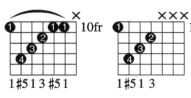

1 b5 1 3 b5 1   1 b5 1 3   1 3 b5 1

A°

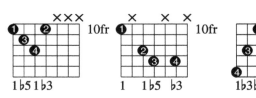

1 b5 1 b3   1 1 b5 b3   1 b3 b5 1

A5

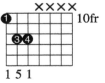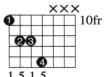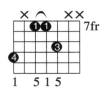

1 5 1   1 5 1 5   1 5 1 5

Aadd9

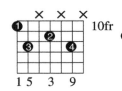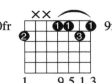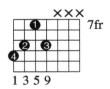

1 5 3 9   1   9 5 1 3   1 3 5 9

Am(add9)

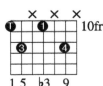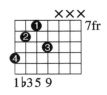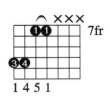

1 5 b3 9   1 5 9 b3   1 b3 5 9

Asus4

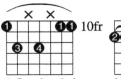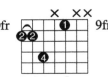

1 5 4 1 4   1 4 1 5   1 4 5 1

Asus2

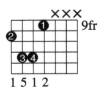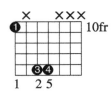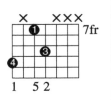

1 5 1 2   1 2 5   1 5 2

A6

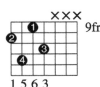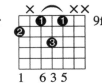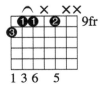

1 5 6 3   1 6 3 5   1 3 6 5

Am6

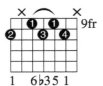 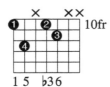 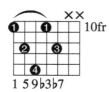

1 6♭3 5 1   1 5 ♭3 6   1♭3 6   5

Amaj7

 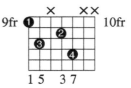 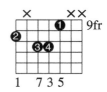

1 1 3 5 7 3   1 5   3 7   1 7 3 5

Amaj7♯5

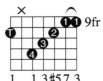 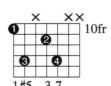 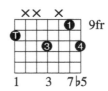 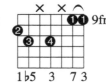 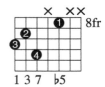

1 1 3 ♯5 7 3   1♯5   3 7   1 3 7   ♯5

Amaj7♭5

 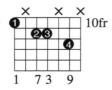 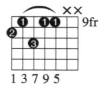 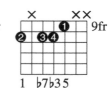

1   3 7♭5   1♭5 3 7 3   1 3 7   ♭5

Amaj9

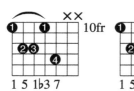 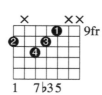

1 5   9 5 7 3   1 7 3 9   1 3 7 9 5

Am7

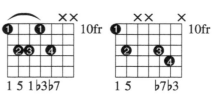 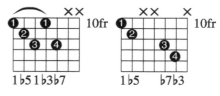 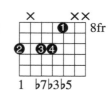

1 5 1♭3♭7   1 5   ♭7♭3   1 ♭7♭3 5

Am(maj7)

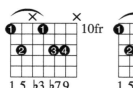 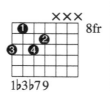 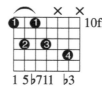

1 5 1♭3 7   1 5   7♭3   1 7♭3 5

Am7♭5

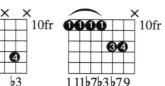 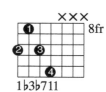

1♭5 1♭3♭7   1♭5 ♭7♭3   1 ♭7♭3♭5

Am9

1 5 ♭3 ♭7 9   1 5 9♭3♭7   1♭3♭7 9

Am11

1 5♭7 11 ♭3   1 11♭7♭3♭7 9   1♭3♭7 11

A7

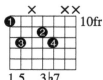 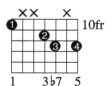 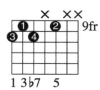

1 5 3♭7   1   3♭7 5   1 3♭7 5

A7sus4

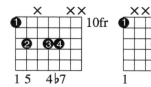 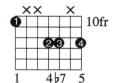 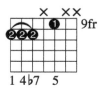

1 5 4♭7   1   4♭7 5   1 4♭7 5

A+7

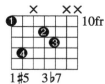 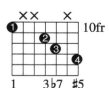 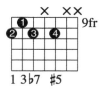

1 #5 3♭7   1   3♭7 #5   1 3♭7 #5

A7♭5

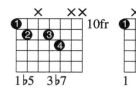 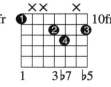 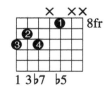

1♭5 3♭7   1   3♭7 ♭5   1 3♭7 ♭5

A9

 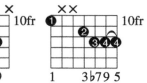 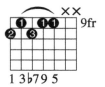

1 5♭7 3 9   1   3♭7 9 5   1 3♭7 9 5

A7#9

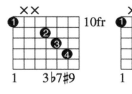 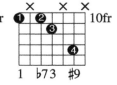 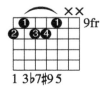

1   3♭7#9   1   ♭7 3   #9   1 3♭7#9 5

A7♭9

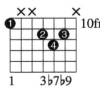 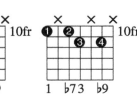 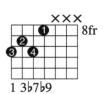

1   3♭7♭9   1   ♭7 3   ♭9   1 3♭7♭9

A11

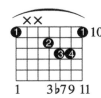 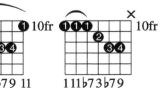 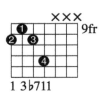

1   3♭7 9 11   1 11♭7 3♭7 9   1 3♭7 11

A13

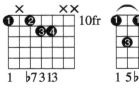 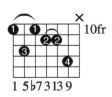

1 ♭7 3 13   1 5♭7 3 13 9   1 3♭7 9 13

A°7

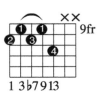 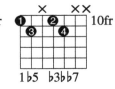 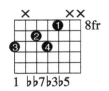

1♭5♭♭7♭3   1♭5 ♭3♭♭7   1 ♭♭7♭3♭5

B♭

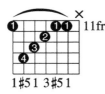
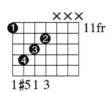
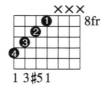

B♭m

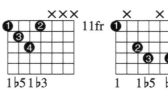
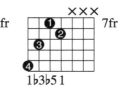

B♭+

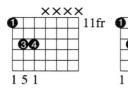
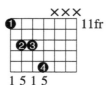
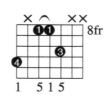

B♭°

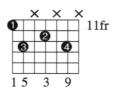
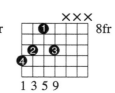

B♭5

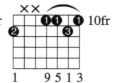

B♭add9

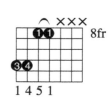

B♭m(add9)

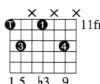
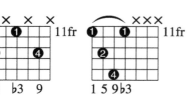
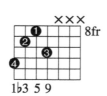
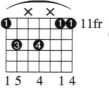
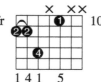

B♭sus4

B♭sus2

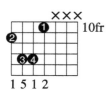
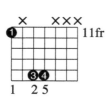
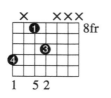

B♭6

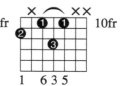
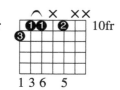

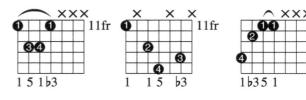
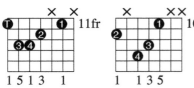

B♭m6

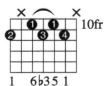

1   6 b3 5 1   1 5   b3 6   1 b3 6   5

B♭maj7

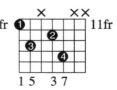

1   1 3 5 7 3   1 5   3 7   1   7 3 5

B♭maj7♯5

1   1 3 ♯5 7 3   1 ♯5   3 7   1 3 7   ♯5

B♭maj7♭5

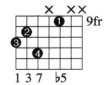

1   3   7 b5   1 b5   3   7 3   1 3 7   b5

B♭maj9

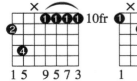

1 5   9 5 7 3   1   7 3   9   1 3 7 9 5

B♭m7

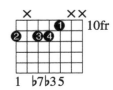

1 5   1 b3 b7   1 5   b7 b3   1   b7 b3 5

B♭m(maj7)

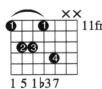

1 5   1 b3 7   1 5   7 b3   1   7 b3 5

B♭m7♭5

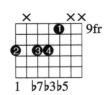

1 b5 1 b3   b7   1 b5   b7 b3   1   b7 b3 b5

B♭m9

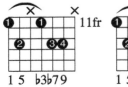

1 5   b3 b7 9   1 5   9 b3 b7   1 b3 b7 9

B♭m11

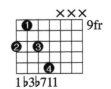

1   5 b7 11   b3   1 11 b7 b3 b7 9   1 b3 b7 11

Bb7

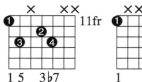

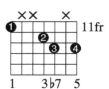

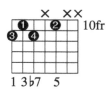

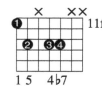

Bb7sus4

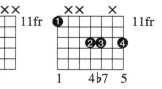

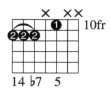

Bb+7

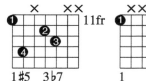

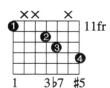

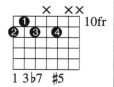

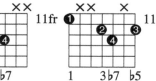

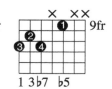

Bb7b5

Bb9

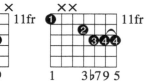

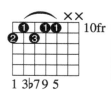

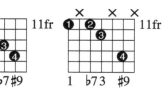

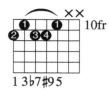

Bb7#9

Bb7b9

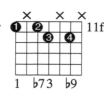

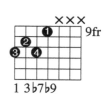

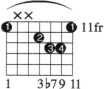

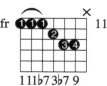

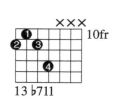

Bb11

Bb13

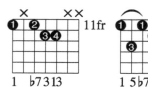

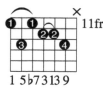

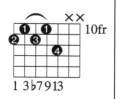

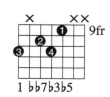

Bb°7

40

B

B

1 5 1 5 1 3

1 1 5 3

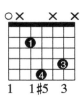
1 3 5 1   9fr

Bm

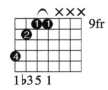
1 5 1 5 1b3   1 1 5 b3   1b3 5 1   9fr

B+

1 1 3 #5 1 #5

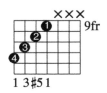
1 1 #5 3

1 3 #5 1   9fr

B°

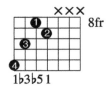
1 1b5 1b3   1 1 1b3b5   1b3b5 1   8fr

B5

1 5 1

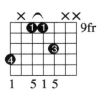
1 5 1 5 1

1 5 1 5   9fr

Badd9

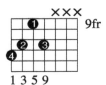
1 1 3 9 5   1 5 3 9   1 3 5 9   9fr

Bm(add9)

1 1b3 9 5

1 5b3 9

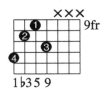
1b3 5 9   9fr

Bsus4

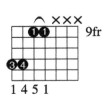
1 1 5 1 4   1 5 1 4 1   1 4 5 1   9fr

Bsus2

1 1 5 1 2 5

1 5 2

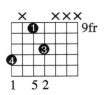
1 5 2   9fr

B6

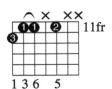
1 1 3 6 1 5   1 6 1 3   1 3 6 5   11fr

Bm6

1 1b3 6 1 5   1 6 1b3   1b3 6 5

Bmaj7

  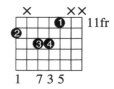

1 5 1 5 7 3   1 1 3 7 1 5   1 7 3 5

Bmaj7#5

 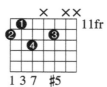

1 1#5 7 3   1 1 3 7 1#5   1 3 7 #5

Bmaj7b5

  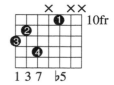

1 1b5 7 3   1 1 3 7 1b5   1 3 7 b5

Bmaj9

  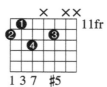

1 1 3 7 9   1 5 9 3 7   1 3 7 9 5

Bm7

  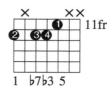

1 5 b7 b3 b7 b3 5   1 1 5 b7 b3   1 b7 b3 5

Bm(maj7)

 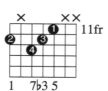

1 1b3 7 1 5   1 1 5 7 b3   1 7 b3 5

Bm7b5

  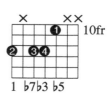

1 1b3 b7 1 b5   1 1b5 b7 b3   1 b7 b3 b5

Bm9

1 1b3 b7 9 5   1 5 9 b3 b7   1b3 b7 9

Bm11

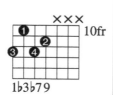 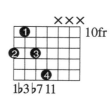

1 1b3 b7 1 11   1 5 11 b7 b3   1b3 b7 11

B7

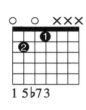

1   1 3♭7 1 5   1 5♭7 3   1 3♭7   5   11fr

B7sus4

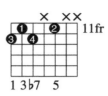

1   1 4♭7 1 4   1   5♭7 4   1 4♭7   5   11fr

B+7

1   1 3♭7 1 ♯5   1   1♯5♭7 3   1 3♭7   ♯5   11fr

B7♭5

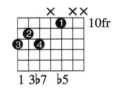

1   1 3♭7 1 ♭5   1   1♭5♭7 3   1 3♭7   ♭5   10fr

B9

1   1 3♭7 9 5   1 5♭7 3   9   1 3♭7 9 5   11fr

B7♯9

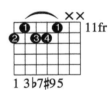

1   1 3♭7 ♯9   1 5♭7 3   ♯9   1 3♭7♯9 5   11fr

B7♭9

1   1 3♭7♭9   1 5♭7 3   ♭9   1 3♭7♭9   10fr

B11

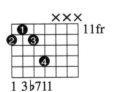

1   1 3♭7 9 11   1 5♭7 3   9 11   1 3♭7 11   11fr

B13

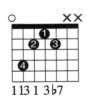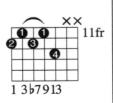

1 5♭7 3 13   1 13 1   3♭7   1 3♭7 9 13   11fr

B°7

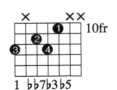

1   1♭3♭♭7 1♭5   1   1♭5♭♭7 3   1   ♭♭7 3♭5   10fr

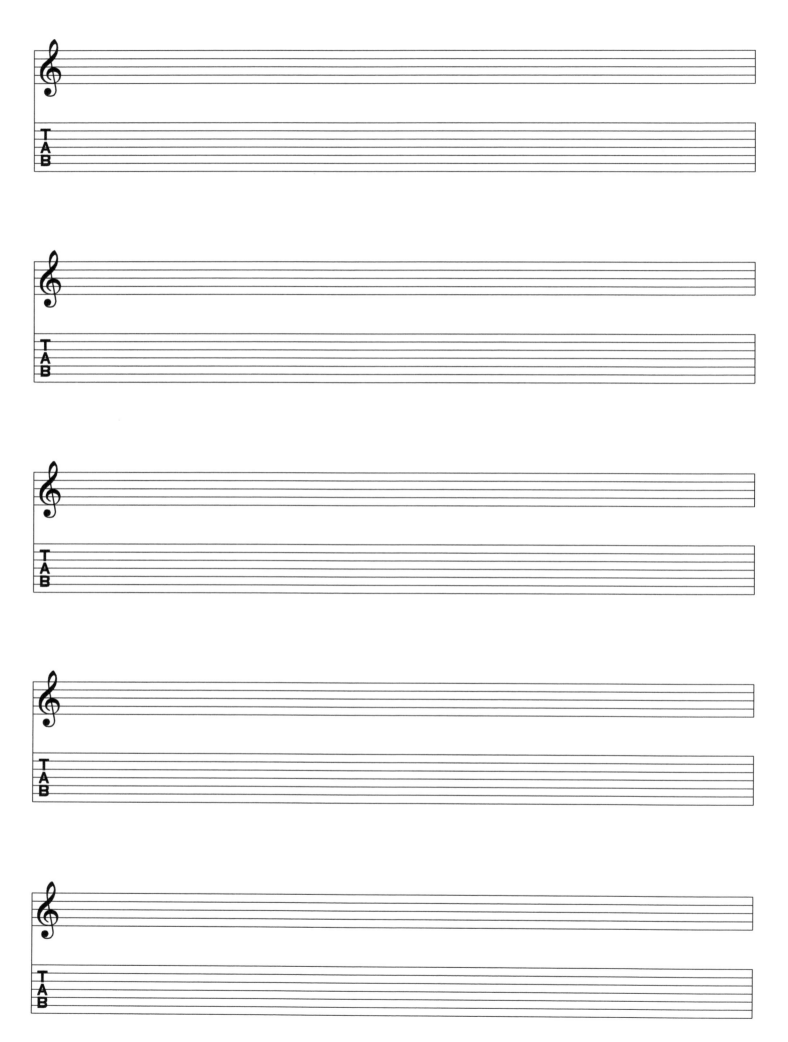

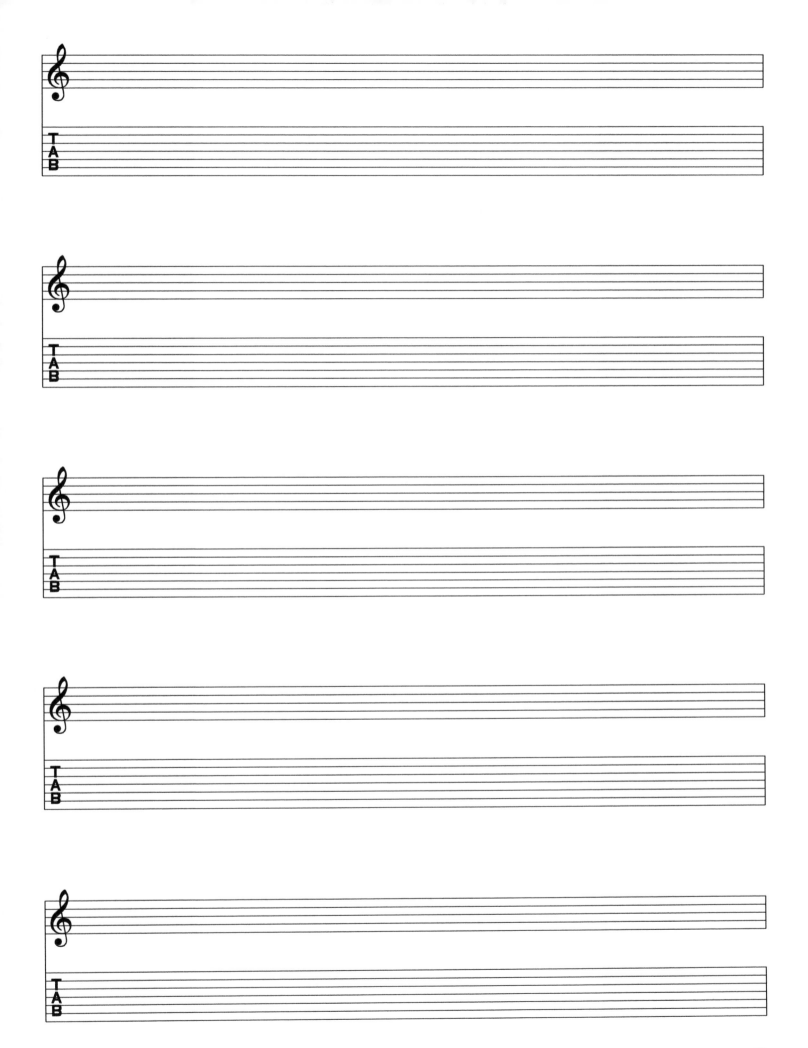

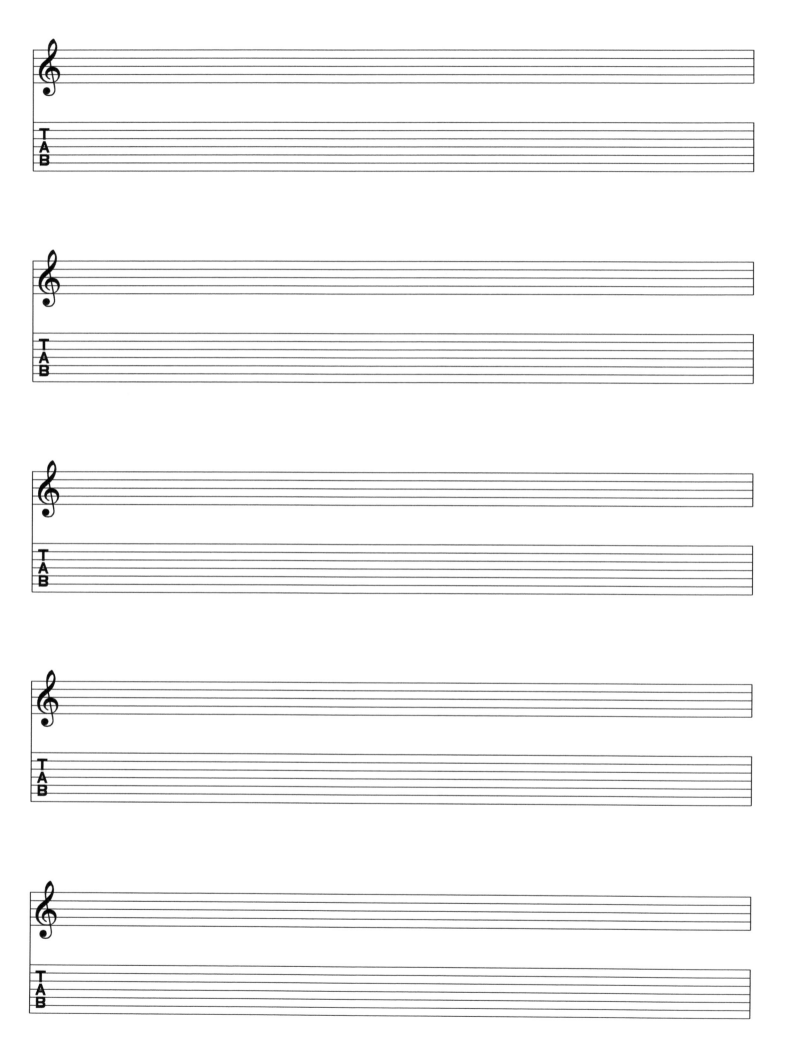

Get Better at Guitar

...with these Great Guitar Instruction Books from Hal Leonard!

101 GUITAR TIPS
INCLUDES TAB

STUFF ALL THE PROS KNOW AND USE

by Adam St. James

This book contains invaluable guidance on everything from scales and music theory to truss rod adjustments, proper recording studio set-ups, and much more.

00695737 Book/Online Audio $16.99

AMAZING PHRASING
INCLUDES TAB

by Tom Kolb

This book/audio pack explores all the main components necessary for crafting well-balanced rhythmic and melodic phrases. It also explains how these phrases are put together to form cohesive solos. The companion audio contains 89 demo tracks, most with full-band backing.

00695583 Book/Online Audio $19.99

ARPEGGIOS FOR THE MODERN GUITARIST
INCLUDES TAB

by Tom Kolb

Using this no-nonsense book with online audio, guitarists will learn to apply and execute all types of arpeggio forms using a variety of techniques, including alternate picking, sweep picking, tapping, string skipping, and legato.

00695862 Book/Online Audio $19.99

BLUES YOU CAN USE

by John Ganapes

This comprehensive source for learning blues guitar is designed to develop both your lead and rhythm playing. Includes: 21 complete solos • blues chords, progressions and riffs • turnarounds • movable scales and soloing techniques • string bending • utilizing the entire fingerboard • and more.

00142420 Book/Online Media...................$19.99

CONNECTING PENTATONIC PATTERNS
INCLUDES TAB

by Tom Kolb

If you've been finding yourself trapped in the pentatonic box, this book is for you! This hands-on book with online audio offers examples for guitar players of all levels, from beginner to advanced. Study this book faithfully, and soon you'll be soloing all over the neck with the greatest of ease.

00696445 Book/Online Audio $19.99

FRETBOARD MASTERY
INCLUDES TAB

by Troy Stetina

Untangle the mysterious regions of the guitar fretboard and unlock your potential. This book familiarizes you with all the shapes you need to know by applying them in real musical examples, thereby reinforcing and reaffirming your newfound knowledge.

00695331 Book/Online Audio $19.99

GUITAR AEROBICS
INCLUDES TAB

by Troy Nelson

Here is a daily dose of guitar "vitamins" to keep your chops fine tuned! Musical styles include rock, blues, jazz, metal, country, and funk. Techniques taught include alternate picking, arpeggios, sweep picking, string skipping, legato, string bending, and rhythm guitar.

00695946 Book/Online Audio $19.99

GUITAR CLUES
INCLUDES TAB

OPERATION PENTATONIC

by Greg Koch

Whether you're new to improvising or have been doing it for a while, this book/audio pack will provide loads of delicious licks and tricks that you can use right away, from volume swells and chicken pickin' to intervallic and chordal ideas.

00695827 Book/Online Audio $19.99

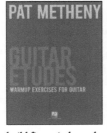

PAT METHENY – GUITAR ETUDES
INCLUDES TAB

Over the years, in many master classes and workshops around the world, Pat has demonstrated the kind of daily workout he puts himself through. This book includes a collection of 14 guitar etudes he created to help you limber up, improve picking technique and build finger independence.

00696587...$15.99

PICTURE CHORD ENCYCLOPEDIA

This comprehensive guitar chord resource for all playing styles and levels features five voicings of 44 chord qualities for all twelve keys – 2,640 chords in all! For each, there is a clearly illustrated chord frame, as well as *an actual photo* of the chord being played!

00695224...$19.99

RHYTHM GUITAR 365
INCLUDES TAB

by Troy Nelson

This book provides 365 exercises – one for every day of the year! – to keep your rhythm chops fine tuned. Topics covered include: chord theory; the fundamentals of rhythm; fingerpicking; strum patterns; diatonic and non-diatonic progressions; triads; major and minor keys; and more.

00103627 Book/Online Audio $24.99

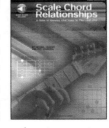

SCALE CHORD RELATIONSHIPS
INCLUDES TAB

by Michael Mueller & Jeff Schroedl

This book/audio pack explains how to: recognize keys • analyze chord progressions • use the modes • play over nondiatonic harmony • use harmonic and melodic minor scales • use symmetrical scales • incorporate exotic scales • and much more!

00695563 Book/Online Audio $14.99

SPEED MECHANICS FOR LEAD GUITAR
INCLUDES TAB

by Troy Stetina

Take your playing to the stratosphere with this advanced lead book which will help you develop speed and precision in today's explosive playing styles. Learn the fastest ways to achieve speed and control, secrets to make your practice time really count, and how to open your ears and make your musical ideas more solid and tangible.

00699323 Book/Online Audio $19.99

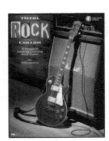

TOTAL ROCK GUITAR
INCLUDES TAB

by Troy Stetina

This comprehensive source for learning rock guitar is designed to develop both lead and rhythm playing. It covers: getting a tone that rocks • open chords, power chords and barre chords • riffs, scales and licks • string bending, strumming, and harmonics • and more.

00695246 Book/Online Audio $19.99

Guitar World Presents
STEVE VAI'S GUITAR WORKOUT
INCLUDES TAB

In this book, Steve Vai reveals his path to virtuoso enlightenment with two challenging guitar workouts – one 10-hour and one 30-hour – which include scale and chord exercises, ear training, sight-reading, music theory, and much more.

00119643...$14.99

HAL•LEONARD®

Order these and more publications from your favorite music retailer at
halleonard.com

1020
032